how2become

KS3 ENGLISH IS EASY

(READING – THE BASICS)

THE
REVISION
SERIES

www.How2Become.com

As part of this product you have also received FREE access to online tests that will help you to pass Key Stage 3 ENGLISH
(Reading – The Basics).

To gain access, simply go to:

www.PsychometricTestsOnline.co.uk

Get more products
for passing any test at:

www.How2Become.com

Orders: Please contact How2Become Ltd, Suite 14, 50 Churchill Square Business Centre, Kings Hill, Kent ME19 4YU.

You can order through Amazon.co.uk under ISBN 9781910602973, via the website www.How2Become.com or through Gardners.com.

ISBN: 9781910602973

First published in 2016 by How2Become Ltd.

Typeset for How2Become Ltd by Anton Pshinka.

Disclaimer

CONTENTS

THE
REVISION
SERIES

UNDERSTANDING THE CURRICULUM

THE NATIONAL CURRICULUM

State-funded school pupils are taught a curriculum of 'core' subjects. These core subjects teach them skills which are paramount to creating well-rounded and educated citizens.

In Key Stage 3 (ages 11-14), the core subjects that must be taught in schools include the following:

- **English**
- **Maths**
- **Science**
- **Art and Design**
- **Citizenship**
- **Computing**
- **Design and Technology**
- **Languages**
- **Geography**
- **History**
- **Music**
- **Physical Education**

All schools, from Key Stage 1 to Key Stage 4, must also teach Religious Studies to their students; and from the age of 11, children will also be taught Sex Education. However, parents are given the option of pulling their children from Religious Studies and Sex Education lessons.

THE IMPORTANCE OF ENGLISH

Students are taught English via spoken language, reading, writing and vocabulary. Not only is this a core subject which all students are required to undertake, but this subject is an integral part of other school subjects. Children will need to have a strong grasp of the English language, and this will prove vital if they are to be successful across their other school subjects.

The fundamental aims of the English subject include:

- Reading with fluency and ease;
- Demonstrating a good understanding of the English language;
- Highlighting the importance of reading, and allowing students to read for both pleasure and academia;
- Learning to appreciate the English language and its heritage;
- Acquiring a strong English vocabulary; to improve students' ability in reading, writing and listening;
- Practising how to write effective literature, adapting their writing and language with a purpose, context and audience in mind;
- Improving children's confidence in their English abilities, allowing them to become competent in the English language via verbal and written communication.

In Key Stage 3, the English subject focuses on four main 'disciplines':

- **Reading;**
- **Writing;**
- **Grammar and Vocabulary;**
- **Spoken English.**

The aforementioned disciplines are all used in order to teach students vital skills for both academia and the outside world.

READING AND WRITING

Reading and writing are extremely important basic skills, which every person should gain from an early age.

The ability to read is necessary across other school subjects too, and therefore it is important that students are able to read fluently and effectively.

Writing is another great skill, which can be altered to reflect different contexts, purposes and audiences. In Key Stage 3, students are required to write different literary texts, for different purposes. Thus, this requires a strong level of vocabulary and grammar.

GRAMMAR AND VOCABULARY

Students in Key Stage 3 will need to build upon knowledge which was obtained in Key Stage 2.

Teachers will need to enhance students' knowledge, by teaching them the importance of grammar, punctuation and spelling. These key areas allow students to not only analyse literary texts, but also improve their own writing style.

Linguistically, students will need to develop a strong understanding of English terminology, and learn how this can be applied to literary texts. This includes learning how to use appropriate vocabulary and understanding the meaning of words and phrases; as well as learning the ability to analyse, practice and apply literary techniques to their own work.

SPOKEN ENGLISH

Not only is written communication an important aspect of the English language, but the ability to speak fluent English is just as vital.

Spoken English is used every day, in a range of different contexts. Developing a person's speaking skills will allow for well-rounded citizens, who have the ability to communicate effectively.

Speaking skills allow students to become more confident at speaking out loud, and to engage with the English language competently.

Having a strong understanding of the English language will allow students to become fluent in written and spoken English. This will allow them to communicate effectively with the world around them, thus allowing children to become engaged in cultural, social and economic issues, and intellectual debates.

ENGLISH SUBJECT CONTENT

Below I have broken down the aims and objectives of each 'discipline' for the subject. This will hopefully give you some idea of what will be assessed, and how you can improve different areas in your reading, writing and speaking abilities.

READING

Pupils will be taught how to:

❏ Develop an appreciation of the English language.
❏ Engage with a variety of literary texts including:
  - *Non-fiction, fiction, plays and poetry. Texts that cover a wide range of genres, eras, authors, styles and narratives.*
  - *Reading books for pleasure and academia.*
  - *Understanding the importance of Shakespeare's works.*
❏ Engage with challenging texts by:
  - *Learning new vocabulary, grammar and literary techniques.*
  - *Analysing key words and phrases.*
  - *Making inferences and assumptions based on the information provided.*
  - *Knowing the meaning behind the text, including the purpose, audience and context.*
❏ Read critically:
  - *Recognising different literary techniques.*
  - *Analysing narration, characterisation, style, themes and genre.*
  - *Comparing two or more texts (cross-examination).*
  - *Understanding meaning through figurative language, word choices, structure and conventions.*

WRITING

<u>Pupils will be taught how to:</u>

❑ Write with fluency, ease and control.
❑ Write a range of different literary texts including:
  ▪ *Strong, persuasive, narrative essays.*
  ▪ *Short stories, plays, poetry.*
  ▪ *Imaginative writing.*
  ▪ *Formal letters.*
  ▪ *Scripts and presentations.*
❑ Plan, draft and proofread writing:
  ▪ *Plan and draft your ideas. Think about:*
    o *Characters, narrative, themes, motives, style, context, audience, purpose.*
  ▪ *Carefully choosing grammar and understanding the importance of vocabulary.*
  ▪ *Structuring your writing format in a clear and concise manner.*
  ▪ *Understanding the importance of audience, and how your writing can be influential.*
❑ Be original and creative.
❑ Use the English language in a way that is expressive, creative, informative, imaginative or personal.

SPOKEN ENGLISH

<u>Pupils will be taught how to:</u>

❑ Verbally communicate to a high standard by:
  ▪ *Speaking confidently, persuasively and effectively.*
❑ Improve their speaking skills by engaging with particular grammar and vocabulary:
  ▪ *Understanding what type of spoken English you should use and in what context.*
  ▪ *Understanding how to get your point across in the best possible way.*
❑ Participate in verbal debates, discussions and presentations.
❑ Improve on speaking skills such as volume, tone, enthusiasm and interaction.

GRAMMAR AND VOCABULARY

Pupils will be taught how to:

☐ Improve on pre-existing grammar and vocabulary skills taught in Key Stage 2.
☐ Understand the importance of grammar:
   - *How this creates meaning.*
   - *The impact this has on the audience.*
☐ Analyse key words and phrases:
   - *Why they are used.*
   - *The meaning behind them.*
   - *What is the author implying/inferring?*
☐ Understand what grammar and vocabulary to use. Think about:
   - *What kind of literary text you are writing/reading.*
   - *What do words mean and how can they be interpreted?*
   - *Is it a formal or informal piece of literary text?*

English is not only a core subject, but a topic that impacts upon every aspect of our daily lives. As you can see, it is imperative that students are able to engage with the English language, in order to develop key life skills.

USING THIS GUIDE

This guide focuses specifically on Key Stage 3 English Reading (The Basics). This book will focus on the basics that every child will need to know, to ensure top marks in English reading.

HOW WILL I BE ASSESSED?

In Years 7, 8 and 9, children will be assessed based on Levels. These 3 years do not count towards anything, and are simply a reflection of progression and development. Key Stage 3 (Years 7, 8 and 9) are schooling years which determine whether or not pupils are meeting the minimum requirements. These 3 years are integral for preparing pupils for their GCSEs (which will begin in Year 10).

Although these years do not count towards any final results, they do go a long way to deciphering which GCSEs you will pick up in Year 10. For example, if you were excelling in Art and Design in KS3, you could consider taking this subject at GCSE. The subjects that you choose at GCSE will impact upon your future aspirations, including further education and career opportunities.

You will be monitored and assessed throughout these schooling years, via the following:

- Ongoing teacher assessments;
- Term progress reports;
- Summative assessments at the end of each academic year.

By the end of Key Stage 3, pupils are expected to achieve Levels 5 or 6.

THE
REVISION
SERIES

INCREASE YOUR CHANCES

Below is a list of GOLDEN NUGGETS that will help YOU and your CHILD to prepare for the Key Stage 3 English.

Golden Nugget 1 – Revision timetables

When it comes to revising, preparation is key. That is why you need to sit down with your child and come up with an efficient and well-structured revision timetable.

It is important that you work with your child to assess their academic strengths and weaknesses, in order to carry out these revision sessions successfully.

TIP – Focus on their weaker areas first!

TIP – Create a weekly revision timetable to work through different subject areas.

TIP – Spend time revising with your child. Your child will benefit from your help and this is a great way for you to monitor their progress.

Golden Nugget 2 – Understanding the best way your child learns

There are many different ways to revise when it comes to exams, and it all comes down to picking a way that your child will find most useful.

Below is a list of the common learning styles that you may want to try with your child:

- **Visual** – the use of pictures and images to remember information.

- **Aural** – the use of sound and music to remember information.

- **Verbal** – the use of words, in both speech and writing, to understand information.

- **Social** – working together in groups.

- **Solitary** – working and studying alone.

Popular revision techniques include: *mind mapping, flash cards, making notes, drawing flow charts,* and *diagrams.* You could instruct your child on how to turn diagrams and pictures into words, and words into diagrams. Try as many different methods as possible, to see which style your child learns from the most.

TIP – Work out what kind of learner your child is. What method will they benefit from the most?

TIP – Try a couple of different learning aids and see if you notice a change in your child's ability to understand what is being taught.

Golden Nugget 3 – Break times

Allow your child plenty of breaks when revising.

It's really important not to overwork your child.

TIP – Practising for 10 to 15 minutes per day will improve your child's reading ability.

TIP – Keep in mind that a child's retention rate is usually between 30 to 50 minutes. Any longer than this, and your child may start to lose interest.

Golden Nugget 4 – Practice, practice and more practice!

Purchase past practice papers. Although the curriculum will have changed for 2016, practice papers are still a fantastic way for you to gain an idea of how your child is likely to be tested.

Golden Nugget 5 – Variety is key!

Make sure that your child reads a VARIETY of different literary texts. Broadening their understanding of different genres, styles and formats will help them prepare effectively for reading comprehension.

> *TIP – Take your child to a library and let them discover different types of books. This will greatly increase their understanding of different literary styles.*

Golden Nugget 6 – Improve their confidence

Encourage your child to communicate verbally, as well as in written formats. This will allow them to improve their confidence and improve their spoken English.

> *TIP – Have discussions and debates in order to encourage your child to open up and discuss their views.*
>
> *TIP – Try and get your child to deliver presentations to family members and friends. This will really help to improve their confidence.*

Golden Nugget 7 – Stay positive!

The most important piece of preparation advice we can give you, is to make sure that your child is positive and relaxed about their assessments.

Don't let exams worry you, and certainly don't let them worry your child.

> *TIP – Make sure the home environment is as comfortable and relaxed as possible for your child.*

Golden Nugget 8 – Answer the easier questions first

A good tip to teach your child is to answer all the questions they find easiest first. That way, they can swiftly work through the paper, before attempting the questions they struggle with.

TIP – Get your child to undergo a practice paper. Tell them to fill in the answers that they find the easiest first. That way, you can spend time helping your child with the questions they find more difficult.

Spend some time working through the questions they find difficult and make sure that they know how to work out the answer.

Golden Nugget 9 – Make sure they refer back to the text

One of the biggest mistakes a child can make in their reading test, is that they don't refer back to the text. All of the answers can be found in the text, therefore they should support their answers with information taken from the passage, as opposed to relying on their memory.

Golden Nugget 10 – Understanding key terms

The next section is a glossary containing all the KEY TERMS that your child should familiarise themselves with.

Sit down with your child and learn as many of these KEY TERMS as you can.

TIP – Why not make your child's learning fun? Write down all of the key terms and cut them out individually. Do the same for the definitions.

Get your child to try and match the KEY TERM with its definition. Keep playing this game until they get them all right!

Golden Nugget 11 – Check out our other revision resources

We have a range of other English resources to help you prepare for EVERY element of KS3 English.

LEARN YOU

KEY TERMS

(A to Z)

ADJECTIVE	A 'describing' word. A word used to describe how something looks, feels, smells or tastes. Adjectives also tell us how someone is feeling. *Example 1 – An **early** start* *Example 2 – A **large** spider*
ADVERB	Adverbs are words that describe a verb. These words tend to tell us how something or someone is doing, or what they are doing. *Example 1 – The boy walked **slowly*** *Example 2 – He **gracefully** took her hand*
ANTONYM	An antonym refers to a word which has the **opposite** meaning to another. *Example 1 – **Soft** is the antonym of **hard*** *Example 2 – **Up** is the antonym of **down***
APOSTROPHE (')	An apostrophe is a punctuation mark used to (1) indicate belonging or (2) indicate the omission of letters. *Example 1 – Katie's bedroom, Joe's homework* *Example 2 – didn't (did not), can't (cannot), I'm (I am)*
AUDIENCE	The people who view the text.
CHARACTERISATION	The way in which a character is conveyed. Characterisation is the way in which people speak, behave and look.
CLAUSE	A clause is part of a sentence that contains a verb and a subject. *Example 1 – Peter **tackles** (verb) **Jason** (subject)* *Example 2 – Mikey **piggybacks** Jackie*
CLOSE READING	A close, intense reading of a text.

COLON **(:)**	A punctuation mark used to (1) join sentences, (2) introduce lists, (3) introduce a quotation or (4) introduce explanations. *Example 1 – Here is my shopping list: bread, milk, eggs* *Example 2 – Tim was feeling tired: he didn't sleep very well last night*
COMMA **(,)**	A punctuation mark used to indicate (1) a pause between parts of sentences or (2) separating items in list format. *Example 1 – On Tuesday, it was raining* *Example 2 – At the shop, I bought a sausage roll, a packet of crisps, an orange and a chocolate bar*
COMPARING TEXTS	Comparing two or more literary texts, to analyse the similarities and differences.
CONJUNCTION	A conjunction is a word that joins phrases or words together. *Example 1 – I don't like pizza **or** pasta* *Example 2 – Fred loves golf **and** football*
CONTEXT	Historical or cultural context. Understanding the context behind the written text.
CONTRACTION	Contractions are 'shorthand' ways of writing words. It is one word usually made up of two words. *Example 1 – **you've** (you have)* *Example 2 – **doesn't** (does not)*
CRITICAL READING	Reading a text and undergoing critical analysis.
DASH **(–)**	A dash is used to separate information. It is stronger than a comma, but not as formal as a colon. Not to be confused with a hyphen (a dash line is longer).

DETERMINER	A determiner is a word that goes before a noun in order to clarify it. *Example 1 – The party is at **my** house* *Example 2 – I teach a **one** day training course*
ELLIPSIS **(...)**	An ellipsis is a set of three dots (full stops) which can add suspense, leave a sentence hanging or show interruptions or missing words. *Example 1 – Josie stepped outside her front door, when all of a sudden...* *Example 2 – She was without hope... empty...*
EXCLAMATION MARK **(!)**	An exclamation mark is used to show a command or something that is forceful or surprising. *Example 1 – Ouch!* *Example 2 – That really hurt!*
FIGURATIVE LANGUAGE	A way of creating imagery through the use of metaphors, similes, hyperboles, etc.
FULL STOP **(.)**	A full stop should be used to end a sentence. *Example 1 – The dog runs across the road.* *Example 2 – Sam likes peanuts.*
HOMONYMS	These are words that *sound* and are spelled the same, but have different meanings. *Example 1 – **watch** (to watch something) or a watch (to tell the time)* *Example 2 – **fair** (fair skinned) or fair (it's not fair)*
HOMOPHONES	These are words that *sound* the same but are spelt differently, and have different meanings. *Example 1 – **to, too, two*** *Example 2 – **they're, their, there***

INVERTED COMMAS (" ")	Inverted commas are used to show direct speech or quotation. These can either be single (') or double ("). Inverted commas can also be used to draw attention to something unusual, ironic or arguably incorrect. *Example 1 – "What time does the lesson start?"* *Example 2 – Gareth said, "I like theme parks"*
LANGUAGE	The words and vocabulary used in a literary text.
NARRATIVE	The storyline and/or meaning of a text.
NOUN	A word that names something. *Examples – Hannah, London, forest, wolf*
PLURAL	More than one of something. *Example – toys, teeth, lives, babies*
PREFIX	A prefix is added to the beginning of a word to make a new word. *Example 1 – **dis**regard, **dis**belief* *Example 2 – **un**natural, **un**happy*
PREPOSITION	A preposition tells us where something is or how they are related. *Examples – under, over, before, beside, between, near, beyond, past, from, on top of*
PRONOUN	A word that replaces the noun. *Examples – I, me, she, him, they, which, who, ours, yours, its*
PURPOSE	The reasons why a text was written. Is it to entertain, inform, instruct, persuade, etc?
QUESTION MARK (?)	A question mark is used to show a question. *Example 1 – What time is it?* *Example 2 – How long are you going to be?*

SCANNING	Quickly reading a text in order to find specific information.
SEMI-COLON **(;)**	A semi-colon is used to separate longer sentences but still reads as one complete sentence. Or to link two closely related sentences. *Example 1 – Polly loves her new trainers; she wears them everywhere* *Example 2 – For Christmas, we spent a day with our grandparents in Ireland; then we spent a day with our aunt and uncle; and then we spent the rest of it back home*
SHAKESPEARE	An English poet and playwright who wrote important sonnets and plays.
SKIMMING	Quickly looking over a text in order to get a general overview of what it is about.
STRUCTURE	The way a literary text is laid out. The structure of a text will depend on what *type* of text it is.
SUFFIX	A suffix is added to the end of the word to make a new word. *Example 1 – charge**able**, manage**able*** *Example 2 – shame**ful**, doubt**ful***
SYNONYM	A word that has the same, or similar, meaning to another word. *Example 1 – pretty = beautiful, stunning, gorgeous* *Example 2 – big = huge, gigantic, enormous, large*
THEMES	The major or subtle ideas that an author explores in the text.
VERB	A verb is a doing or action word. *Example 1 – She **went** to the party* *Example 2 – She **ran** to the shops*

THE
REVISION
SERIES

SKIM, SCAN AND CLOSE READINGS

(Reading Skills)

DIFFERENT WAYS TO READ A TEXT

In order to get the most out of each reading, it's important that you understand how to read a text.

There are several ways in which you can read a text, and each method will allow you to read the text in a different way.

Below I have outlined the three main methods which you can use:

SKIMMING — **1.**

SCANNING — **2.**

CLOSE READING — **3.**

Do you know when you would skim a text, scan a text, or closely read a text?

Each of these different ways of reading are useful in different situations. The method that you use will depend on what you are reading, and what you want to achieve from reading the text.

SKIMMING	SCANNING	CLOSE READING
• Get the 'gist' about the main ideas	• Locate information quickly	• Paying attention to every detail
• Look out for titles, headings and illustrations	• Looking for specific information	• Wanting to know everything that is going on
EXAMPLES Newspapers, websites, articles	**EXAMPLES** Dictionary, TV guide, glossary	**EXAMPLES** Exam papers, instructions, novels

DIFFERENT WAYS TO READ A TEXT

SKIMMING A TEXT

A good technique to get to grips with is **SKIM READING**.

This method involves rapid eye movement across the text, which allows you to understand KEY ideas in the passage.

Skimming involves a number of steps:

STEP 1
Read the title of the text

STEP 2
Read the first paragraph – thoroughly!

STEP 3
Pay attention to the sub-headings

STEP 4
Read the first line of each paragraph

STEP 5
Read the final paragraph completely

- Focus on who, what, when, where, why and how.
- Focus on typographies including boldface, italics, asterisks, underlines etc.
- Focus on unusual wording or phrases.

Skim reading is approximately 1,000 words per minute!

PRACTISING SKIMMING A TEXT

QUESTION

What is the aim of this website?

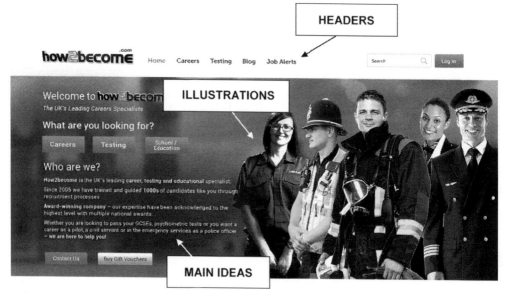

How to answer the question:

- Work out what the question is asking you!

- The question is asking you to work out the aim of website.

- When skimming the page, you will notice the following:

    o Illustration of career people (paramedic, police, firefighter);

    o Headers (careers, courses, testing etc.).

    o Title / Website title (How2become) – suggests the page is all about 'how to become...'

    o Summary – you are able to skim read the main ideas from the short passages on the page.

Make sure when you skim read the text, you actually answer the question. What is the question asking you? What is the 'gist' of the text?

DIFFERENT WAYS TO READ A TEXT

SCANNING A TEXT

Another way you can read a text is by **SCANNING**.

Scanning a text is when you cover a great deal of material, fast, in order to locate specific information.

If you are trying to look for specific key words or phrases, the best way to do this is let your eyes wander over the text and keep a <u>LOOKOUT</u> for what you are trying to find.

<u>Scanning involves a number of steps:</u>

STEP 1
Think to yourself – what are you looking for?

STEP 2
Consider how the information is going to appear

STEP 3
Analyse the layout of the content. Where will it most likely appear?

STEP 4
If it's short, you'll probably scan the whole text. If it's lengthy, you may want to skim read first.

STEP 5
Your eyes should wander over several lines at one time

- In order to scan over a text, you will skip over large amounts of the text in order to find what you are looking for.

- Look out for key words and phrases to help you find the specific information you want.

Scanning is approximately 1,500 or more words per minute!

PRACTISING SCANNING A TEXT

QUESTION

How does the author of this text make you want to visit the holiday park?

> **Recharge your batteries** and enjoy a holiday of tranquillity, peace and stillness. The holiday resort is situated in the Caribbean, and is considered the **'paradise land of dreams'.**
>
> A once in a lifetime opportunity, you can win this **already paid for, all-inclusive holiday for you and three other people.** You'll be enchanted by the people, culture and 24-hour sunshine.
>
> The Caribbean is situated southeast of the Gulf of Mexico and the North American mainland.
>
> With this holiday, you will be able to get involved with the culture, **experience new foods**, lay on the **sandy, white beaches** and wash away your troubles for **14 days.**

How to answer the question:

- Work out what the question is asking you!

- You need to find loads of things in the text that tell you why you should visit the holiday park.

- Some bits of the text will be irrelevant. You should scan through the text quickly and spot key words or phrases that would attract the reader.

- The text in bold signifies some of the main reasons as to why the reader would want to visit the holiday park.

- Make sure the information you pick out is RELEVANT.

Remember, scanning a text means understanding what the question is asking you to do, and then finding that information in the text.

DIFFERENT WAYS TO READ A TEXT

CLOSE READING OF A TEXT

This involves reading a text (like a book, newspaper article or exam paper) in detail to ensure you don't miss anything.

This means you have to focus on all of the grammar and punctuation used. You should also pay attention to sentence structure, conjunctive words and how phrases are used to convey meaning.

Close reading involves a number of steps:

STEP 1
Read the whole text carefully and observe the facts and details provided

STEP 2
Read with a pencil in hand, and annotate the text

STEP 3
Look for patterns. Focus on language, similarities, differences, repetitions etc.

STEP 4
Ask questions about what you have read (focus on how and why)

STEP 5
Ask yourself – what does the author intend?

- Pay attention to everything you read.

- Repetitive readings of the same text will help you to further your critical understanding of the text.

Close reading allows you to analyse the text carefully and in detail.

PRACTISING CLOSE READING OF A TEXT

QUESTION

Reading critically does NOT always mean being negative/critical towards the text.

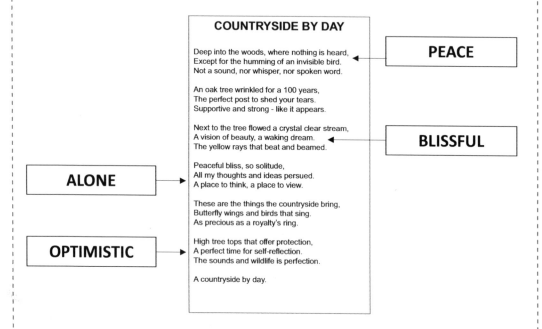

COUNTRYSIDE BY DAY

Deep into the woods, where nothing is heard,
Except for the humming of an invisible bird.
Not a sound, nor whisper, nor spoken word.

PEACE

An oak tree wrinkled for a 100 years,
The perfect post to shed your tears.
Supportive and strong - like it appears.

Next to the tree flowed a crystal clear stream,
A vision of beauty, a waking dream.
The yellow rays that beat and beamed.

BLISSFUL

Peaceful bliss, so solitude,
All my thoughts and ideas persued.
A place to think, a place to view.

ALONE

These are the things the countryside bring,
Butterfly wings and birds that sing.
As precious as a royalty's ring.

High tree tops that offer protection,
A perfect time for self-reflection.
The sounds and wildlife is perfection.

OPTIMISTIC

A countryside by day.

> To read something critically, does NOT always mean negative criticism.

How to answer the question:

- In order to work out the mood, you need to read the whole poem CAREFULLY.

- You need to pay attention to how mood is created using language, narrative, rhythm etc.

- For example, you could pay attention to specific grammar, punctuation and language techniques (similes, metaphors, personification etc.)

Remember, it is important that you pay attention to everything.

POINT, EVIDENCE, EXPLANATION (P.E.E.)

(Reading Skills)

POINT, EVIDENCE, EXPLANATION

UNDERSTANDING THE P.E.E. TECHNIQUE

A great technique to get to grips to improve your reading (and writing) skills, is **P.E.E.**

P.E.E. stands for: Point, Evidence and Explanation. It is a great way to pick out key information from the text, and comment on the text's meaning and purpose.

POINT	Make a point / statement / idea you want to talk about.

- From reading the text, make a point about what you have read. What is the main argument? What is the author trying to do? How does the author make you feel?

EVIDENCE	Support your point using examples / quotations from the text.

- You will need evidence to back up the point you have just made.
- This evidence needs to either be examples or a quote taken from the text.

EXPLAIN	Explain the point you made, and how the evidence supports your answers. Analyse the importance / relevance.

- Explain what the evidence proves.
- Explain why you have made the point, and show how the evidence supports your argument.
- What is the relevance / significance?

POINT, EVIDENCE, EXPLANATION

A STRONG RESPONSE

When using the P.E.E. technique, it is important that you provide strong sentences for each stage.

POINT

- Provide a clear and well structured point.
- It has to show focus.
- It needs to be tailored to the question you're being asked.
- You should use key words from the question in your point.

EXAMPLES
One way that...
It is clear that...
One striking feature of...

EVIDENCE

- Provide short, relevant quotes.
- It needs to be precise and support your point.

EXAMPLES

For example...
This is shown by...
This can be supported...

EXPLAIN

- Explain how the quote supports your point.
- Analyse the evidence.
- Link it back to the question.
- You can show off and add more detail to make your answer stronger.
- Comment on the effect this would have on the reader.
- Link to themes, context, possible interpretations.

EXAMPLES
This shows that...
Clearly...
The use of...
This reinforces that...
The use of the word...

inability

PRACTICE QUESTIONS

> "A merry Christmas, uncle! God save you!" cried a cheerful voice. It was the voice of Scrooge's nephew, who came upon him so quickly that this was the first intimation he had of his approach.
>
> "Bah!" said Scrooge, "Humbug!"
>
> He had so heated himself with rapid walking in the fog and frost, this nephew of Scrooge's, that he was all in a glow; his face was ruddy and handsome; his eyes sparkled, and his breath smoked again. "Christmas a humbug, uncle!" said Scrooge's nephew. "You don't mean that, I am sure?"
>
> "I do," said Scrooge. "Merry Christmas! What right have you to be merry? What reason have you to be merry? You're poor enough."
>
> "Come, then," returned the nephew gaily. "What right have you to be dismal? What reason have you to be morose? You're rich enough."
>
> *A Christmas Carol by Charles Dickens*

Question 1

Using the P.E.E. technique, describe the feelings Scrooge has towards Christmas.

POINT

In this extract Dickens presents Scrooges feelings towards Christmas as frustrated, confused and annoyed

EVIDENCE

This is shown when he states "What right have you be merry? [...] You're poor enough."

EXPLANATION

This reinforces Scrooges feelings, not only is he ~~an~~ frustrated and annoyed at his nephew's inability to ~~understand t~~ understand that Christmas is a 'Hambug.'

For some minutes Alice stood without speaking, looking out in all directions over the country – and a most curious country it was. There were a number of tiny little brooks running straight across it from side to side, and the ground between was divided up into squares by a number of little green hedges, that reached from brook to brook.

'I declare it's marked out just like a large chessboard!' Alice said at last. 'There ought to be some men moving about somewhere – and so there are!' She added in a tone of delight, and her heart began to beat quick with excitement as she went on. 'It's a great huge game of chess that's being played – all over the world – if this *is* the world at all, you know. Oh, what fun it is! How I *wish* I was one of them! I wouldn't mind being a Pawn, if only I might join – though of course I should *like* to be a Queen, best.'

Through the Looking Glass by Lewis Carroll

Question 2

Using the P.E.E. technique, explain how the idea of life as a game is explored.

POINT

In this extract Carroll explores tif the idea of life as a game, and chances

EVIDENCE

This is shown when Alice states "its a great huge game of chess ... all over the world"

EXPLANATION

This suggests to the reader that we are all structured

"It's gone!"

Freddie looked up from peering through one of the glass cabinets, hoping to find the perfect item of jewellery for his best friend, Scarlett. He was in a small jewellery shop in the city centre of CapeTown. The walls were painted in a dark red, with pictures hung crookedly all around. The floor was tiled and scuffed. The harsh lighting made it difficult to see what you were looking at, but somehow it made it feel cosier, more inviting.

Freddie stood in the farthest corner away from the tills, but the sound of the trembling young girl grabbed his attention. No older than 20, the young girl paced around the shop with her phone fixed to her ear, trying to report the incident. As customers stopped in their tracks to ogle the spectacle, the shop was beginning to overflow with curiosity and interest.

Once admired for his vigilance and passion, all Freddie could do now was stand there frozen; contemplating his next move. It had been exactly 3 years. How could he possibly forget it? 3 years since Freddie's accident, and he had found himself in a quandary since that unforgettable day.

"I don't know what happened...one minute it was there, and the next it was gone – the ring is gone".

As moments passed, Freddie knew what had to be done. He couldn't stand by and do nothing. *Come on, you can do it! Just think, think!* He kept reassuring himself, and as he closed his eyes, his body started to tremble. The black nothingness started to get brighter. Reds and oranges began penetrating his vision. These colours then formed distorted images. Images of the ring. *Where, where is it?* Freddie said to himself.

Freddie was known for his excellent vision to read minds and see into the future. However, he had refrained from doing this since his accident, and the feeling of entering this state of mind after so much time made his body go limp.

He opened his eyes, pupils dilated. They were so intense that the strongest gust of wind would not have made him blink. Slowly, Freddie reached into his pocket and pulled out what appeared to be a torch. With his eyes still transfixed, he clicked the button. After a few seconds, he clicked it again.

Now stood there, was a man all in green. A long, silk cape which hovered above the floor, an eye mask that made his eyes look as black as coal, and boots that, although appeared to look 'normal', had hidden features that placed him in a very strong position against all odds.

"It's time...It's time to get back to solving crime!"

Freddie had not realised how loud he said this, and as he turned around, he noticed everyone staring at him, silently. He grinned slightly.

"I've got this..."

Freddie and the Stolen Ring by How2Become

Question 3

Using the P.E.E technique, how is the character of Freddie presented?

For this answer, you should write a detailed paragraph, using the P.E.E. technique to help structure your response. Consider the language used and how the writer draws the reader in.

ANSWERS TO POINT, EVIDENCE AND EXPLANATION

Question 1

The **points** you could have made include:

1. The character of Scrooge is depicted as being quite pessimistic towards Christmas.
2. Scrooge's feelings towards Christmas suggest he has no reason to be merry at Christmas.

The **evidence** you could have used includes:

1. "What right have you to be dismal?"
2. "I do," said Scrooge. "Merry Christmas! What right have you to be merry? What reason have you to be merry? You're poor enough."

The **explanations** you could have made include:

1. This suggests that Scrooge is a gloomy character and is not fond of the idea of Christmas.
2. The fact that Scrooge asks his nephew the reasons why he has to be merry, suggests that Scrooge sees no reason to be happy about Christmas.

Question 2

The **points** you could have made include:

1. The game of chess can be considered as a metaphor for life in general.

The **evidence** you could have used includes:

1. 'It's a great huge game of chess that's being played – all over the world – if this *is* the world at all, you know.

The **explanations** you could have made include:

1. This reinforces the idea that the movements of chess pieces are similar to how people move in their everyday lives. They move around following a certain order and understanding of how the world works.

ple response that would score highly for this question.

t striking features of the text is the author's use of language, in order to create a physical representation of a superhero. The author puts huge emphasis on characteristics mostly associated with superheroes. The author implies that Freddie stood there in "a long, silk cape which hovered above the floor, an eye mask that made his eyes look as black as coal, and boots that, although appeared to look 'normal', had hidden features that placed him in a very strong position against all odds." The dress code reinforces how superheroes would commonly be dressed. The fact that Freddie can also read minds highlights the superpowers he possesses. This allows the reader to visualise the character and depict him as being a superhero; the protagonist of the story.

HOW ARE YOU GETTING ON?

THE
REVISION
SERIES

AUDIENCE, PURPOSE AND CONTEXT

AUDIENCE, PURPOSE AND CONTEXT

There are three main things you need to consider when reading or writing a text:

1. Audience

2. Purpose

3. Context

AUDIENCE

Understanding the audience of a text is important. Who is the text aimed at?

Generally, the term 'audience' refers to people who 'watch' something (like a play or TV programme). However, this term is also used to describe someone who 'reads' something.

An author will need to adjust/tailor their writing in order to be suitable to their audience. The majority of authors will have an intended audience – that means they know who they are hoping to target as their reader.

In order to work out their intended audience, the writer may need to consider the following:

- What kind of text is it?

- How much does the reader already know about the topic?

- What would the reader want to learn from the text?

- What age group will most likely read the text?

- What kind of language will they benefit from the most?

- Is the text based on local, national or world-wide interests?

- What is the overall intention of the text?

AUDIENCE, PURPOSE AND CONTEXT

TYPE OF TEXT AND AUDIENCE

The type of text will depend on who is likely to read it.

TEXT	WHO IS IT AIMED AT?
An English textbook	Students
A picture book	Young children
Young adult fiction	Teenagers
Fishing brochure	Fishing enthusiasts
School reports	Parents/guardians

AUDIENCE, CONTENT, LANGUAGE AND PRESENTATION

Content, language and presentation are also ways in which you can work out the audience of a text.

For example, a fashion magazine is clearly going to appeal to people who take pride in their appearance, and are interested in fashion trends.

A book containing large images, and not much text, suggests that the audience is going to be younger children.

TEXT	WHO IS IT AIMED AT?	CONTENT AND/OR PRESENTATION FEATURES
An English textbook	Students	Technical language, demonstrative images, practice questions
A picture book	Young children	Simple language, large, colourful images, not much text
Young adult fiction	Teenagers	Fast-paced narrative, relatable characters, engaging topics/themes
Fishing brochure	Fishing enthusiasts	Technical language, images, factual information
School reports	Parents/guardians	Grades and comments, addressed to the parent, breakdown of child's progress

AUDIENCE, PURPOSE AND CONTEXT

PURPOSE

Writers don't just write for the sake of it – they have a purpose! They think about what they hope to achieve, and how they want to affect their readers.

There are several purposes of writing:

PURPOSE	EXPLANATION
Instruction	Tell you how to do or make something.
Explanation	Show why or how something happens.
Persuasive	Try to convince the reader to agree with your points. Try to get the reader to do something.
Discussion	Offer alternative points of view on a topic.
Recount	Retell the events or something that has previously happened.
Entertainment	To enjoy a text and fascinate the readers.
Advise	Try to offer advice/opinions to the reader.
Inform	Tell the reader about a particular topic in order to improve their knowledge.
Review	Examine and interpret something in order to offer judgements and opinions.

THE PURPOSE OF THE TEXT AFFECTS THE CONTENT OF THE TEXT

The purpose of a text will affect the content of the text. The writer's choice of language will carefully be chosen in order to serve its particular purpose.

This language will not just emphasise the **purpose**, but it will also use a particular **style** in order to convey that purpose.

For example, a letter to a friend will use simple, informal language, whereas a letter to your employer would be formal (it would need to be professional).

AUDIENCE, PURPOSE AND CONTEXT

TYPE OF LITERARY TEXT

There are a range of different literary texts that all serve different purposes.

The main ones you will need to know are:

- Fiction
- Non-fiction
- Plays
- Poetry

FICTION

Fiction is the creation of stories and ideas. They are created by the IMAGINATION.

These stories are NOT real.

There are many different types of fiction books:

Fantasy	Romance	Horror	Science Fiction (Sci-Fi)
Mystery	Realistic	Historical	Folktales
Adventure	Sports	Humour	Classics

Some fiction stories use more than one **genre**, and this is called a **hybrid**.

By asking questions as you go through, this will allow you to understand what the author was trying to say:

- *How does the author want me to feel at this point?*
- *How does the author feel at this point?*
- *Why have I been provided this information?*
- *What can I learn from the information that has been provided?*
- *Why has the author used a particular phrase?*
- *Who is the narrator of the text and how are they being portrayed?*

AUDIENCE, PURPOSE AND CONTEXT

NON-FICTION

Opposite to fiction, **non-fiction** is writing based on facts and real-life events. This provides readers with information that should be taken as factual and accurate.

TYPES OF NON-FICTION

There are many different *types* of texts that are non-fiction. Each text is written to serve a particular purpose.

NON-FICTION (INSTRUCTION TEXTS)

PURPOSE OF THE TEXT	FEATURES	EXAMPLES
• Instruction texts tell you how to do or make something.	• Step-by-step instructions. • Headers and sub-headings.	• Cookery books. • Instruction manuals.

NON-FICTION (EXPLANATION TEXTS)

PURPOSE OF THE TEXT	FEATURES	EXAMPLES
• Explanation texts provide information on how something happens. • They also discuss why things happen.	• Technical language. • Specific knowledge on a topic. • Diagrams and images that help show what is being spoken about. • Explain processes and effects.	• Life cycles. • Explaining how something works, like a volcano.

NON-FICTION (PERSUASIVE TEXTS)

PURPOSE OF THE TEXT	FEATURES	EXAMPLES
• To try and get the reader to believe a particular view point. • Often based on one point of view. • To inform, to change their minds or encourage them to do something.	• Strong, persuasive language. • Good use of adjectives. • Emotive language. • Repetition.	• Adverts. • Brochures. • TV advertising. • Posters. • Leaflets. • Billboards.

AUDIENCE, PURPOSE AND CONTEXT

NON-FICTION (DISCUSSION TEXTS)

PURPOSE OF THE TEXT	FEATURES	EXAMPLES
• A text that offers alternative points of view. • Discussing an issue or general topic.	• For and against arguments. • Use of emotive language. • The conclusion usually takes one side for either for or against.	• Newspaper articles. • Reviews (book, film, theatre). • Debates.

NON-FICTION (RECOUNT TEXTS)

PURPOSE OF THE TEXT	FEATURES	EXAMPLES
• Recollection of events. • Retelling something that has already happened.	• Introduction and conclusion. • Usually in chronological order.	• Journals. • Diaries. • Write-ups of experiments.

NON-FICTION (NON-CHRONOLOGICAL TEXTS)

PURPOSE OF THE TEXT	FEATURES	EXAMPLES
• To keep a record of information about a specific topic.	• Uses technical language. • Diagrams, photos and illustrations. • Contains factual information about the topic. • Opening statement and conclusion.	• Specific books based on particular subjects. • Encyclopaedias. • Catalogue. • Letter.

Language is a key component when it comes to writing any literary text. The language used in a text will depend on what *type* of non-fiction text it is.

For example:

- A leaflet will use very different language than an extract from a diary. Both are examples of non-fiction texts, but they are both written for a different purpose.

  o A leaflet will often contain facts and use emotional language in order to emphasise a particular point of view.

  o A diary extract is an informal piece of writing which is written from personal experience. This can use informal language such as slang.

AUDIENCE, PURPOSE AND CONTEXT

PLAYS

A play is a form of literature that is written by a **playwright**, which is intended to be **performed** on stage, radio, TV or film.

The layout of a **script** is really important. Apart from looking aesthetically pleasing, it needs to be clear and *look* like a play script.

A PLAY SCRIPT

A script contains TWO main elements in order to convey the style of a play:

Dialogue

- A conversation between characters. In a literary text, the name of the character always appears on the left side of the page, followed by what they say. Each character's dialogue is written on a separate line.

Stage directions

- Instructions for both the actors and director. Usually written in italics or brackets. These instructions tell the actors how to enter the scene, how they should speak or move, and how props need to be used.

See the chapter on William Shakespeare for more information on his plays!

AUDIENCE, PURPOSE AND CONTEXT

POETRY

Poetry is another form of literary writing.

Poems are often written to express feelings, thoughts or ideas. The subject of the poem will depend on what *type* of poem it is.

TYPES OF POETRY

Below is a list of the *types* of poems you will be expected to know for English assessments.

 Sonnet
Lyrical
14 lines
10 syllables to a line
Often about love

 Narrative
Tells a long story
Voice of narrator
or character
Do not have to rhyme

 Tanka
Originate in Japan
5 lines
Syllable count of 5 / 7 / 5 / 7 / 7
Use of similes, metaphors or personification

 Limerick
5 lines
Lines 1, 2 and 5 rhyme
Lines 3 and 4 rhyme
To make you laugh

 Cinquain
5 lines
'Cinq' = 5 in French
Syllable count of 2 / 4 / 6 / 8 / 2

 Couplet
2 lines for a verse
Both lines rhyme

 Haiku
Originate in Japan
3 lines
Syllable count of 5 / 7 / 5
Often about nature

 Acrostic
Word written vertically
Each letter starts sentence
All lines should relate
to the topic of the poem

 Ode
Ancient Greece
Lyric poem
Praise of a person or thing
Deep feelings or emotions

 Free Verse
Follows no rules
Rhythm, syllables, number of lines,
topic = can be anything

Things to consider include: the number of stanzas (paragraphs), language, sound patterns, form and structure.

AUDIENCE, PURPOSE AND CONTEXT

CONTEXT

The context of a text is <u>when</u> and <u>where</u> it was written.

You should consider two contexts:

1. Historical context;

2. Cultural context.

HISTORICAL CONTEXT

The time and era in which a text is written will have a huge effect on the language and style.

Classic fiction uses a different writing style in contrast with modern day texts. This is done on purpose. It uses language codes which help convey the time in which the narrative is set.

> For example, Oliver Twist was written by Charles Dickens, and was published in 1838.
>
> During the 1830s, people were confined to "classes", with the highest being the "gentleman" (who did not have to go off to work).
>
> Dickens presents the idea of poverty and class division. This is conveyed by language codes such as clothing, speech and actions.

Modern day texts still use language codes but to relate to the present day or recent times.

> Modern fiction texts will use different language codes in order to convey different meanings.
>
> These language codes will emphasise that it is written in modern times.
>
> Such language codes to look out for would include:
>
> • Clothing
> • Character style
> • Narrative
> • Themes

AUDIENCE, PURPOSE AND CONTEXT

CULTURAL CONTEXT

Cultural context is another thing to consider when it comes to analysing a text. For this, you would need to think about culture, traditions, society and values.

These will play a huge role in how the text is written, and what the author is trying to convey.

> William Shakespeare wrote Macbeth in 1606. At that time, politics and philosophy are key to this written text.
>
> The political context is significant because it is highlighted in the main themes of the narrative - which is that excessiveness and ambition will have consequences, sooner or later.
>
> The text was written during the reign of King James I. The narrative of Macbeth is extremely dark and cynical.

TO RECAP!

When you read a literary text, you need to pay attention to the following:

- Audience;
- Context;
- Content;
- Purpose.

All of the aforementioned will help you to understand the text in more detail. Remember, all of these are linked to one another.

For example

- The purpose of the text will depend on who reads it and what content is present.
- The context of the text will depend on what the purpose of the text is and who is going to read it.
- The audience of the text will depend on the purpose, context and content.

PRACTICE QUESTIONS

Question 1

Match the type of text with the correct audience.

TEXT   **AUDIENCE**

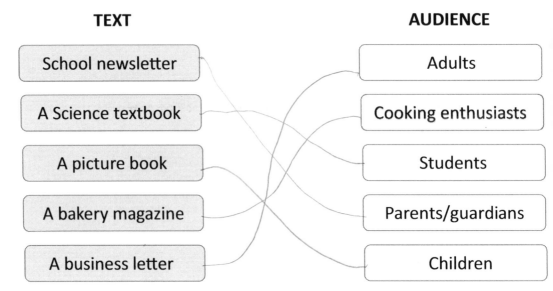

School newsletter   Adults

A Science textbook   Cooking enthusiasts

A picture book   Students

A bakery magazine   Parents/guardians

A business letter   Children

Question 2

The following sentences have been written for different readers. Write down who you think the reader is and explain why you think the text suits each reader. Think about vocabulary and style.

a) Thank you all for taking the time out of your busy schedule for this meeting. It's just a brief talk about the upcoming weeks and what you should be aiming for in terms of work load and deadlines.

AUDIENCE

Adults/workers

EXPLANATION

Someone talking to employers in a proffesional manner

b) At the end of the examination, you will be asked to remain seated and silent for further announcements and until all your booklets are collected. Remain silent until you have left the examination building.

AUDIENCE

Students

EXPLANATION

Examiner explaining the rules of the exams to students and what to do when your time is up. The language/tone shows how serious it is to follow the instructions

c) Last week, a man was sentenced to 3 years in prison for multiple burglaries and one serious attack on a shop assistant. The judge found him guilty and "unremorseful".

AUDIENCE

newsreaders/adults

EXPLANATION

This newspaper article informs readers about ~~otherre~~ current situations regarding multiple burglaries and a serious attack.

Question 3

For the following texts, write what the purpose of each text is.

TEXT	PURPOSE OF TEXT
Cartoon programme	entertain
Weather report	Inform
An advert for a theme park opening	Persuade people
Log book of science experiment	
Debate about school uniforms	Argument
Leaflet on benefits of eating healthily	Advice

Question 4

Using your answers to Question 3, briefly give a definition of the purpose of each text.

a) Cartoon programme

Entertain younger veiwers

b) Weather report

Inform the audience about the weather, whether it be good or bad.

c) An advert for a theme park opening

Persuade people to visit the new theme park.

d) Log book of science experiment

e) The life cycle of a plant

Educate veiwers about the plant life cycle

f) An adult fiction text

Question 5

What would you expect to see on the cover of a magazine entitled 'Film Fanatics'? Describe the purpose of the text, and how this appeals to its specialist audience. Consider content and style.

Question 6

Read the passage carefully and answer the following questions.

'But that was only the effect of the suddenness of your alarm — of the shock. You will not be hysterical again. I dare say we shall have nothing to distress us. I perfectly understand Mr Robinson's directions, and have no fears; and indeed, Mary, I cannot wonder at your husband. Nursing does not belong to a man; it is not his province. A sick child is always the mother's property: her own feelings generally make it so.'

Persuasion by Jane Austen

a) Based on your reading, who do you think the targeted audience is for *Persuasion*?

Some this book is aimed at someone who enjoys classic, & novels old fashioned novels

b) What does this extract suggest about male and female roles, in the time at which this book was set?

Mens roles was to work and provide for the family, whilst womens where to stay home: cooking, cleaning and raise children

c) Explain how Jane Austen contrasts the public domain and domestic domain.

_____

_____

_____

_____

d) Explain how the attitudes in this text do not reflect the same cultural values as modern day society.

Men + women both work, clean, cook and
raise their children, in modern society.

Question 7

There once was a turtle named Joe,

Considered the slowest of the slow.

He entered the race,

With slow as his pace,

On your marks, get set, go!

What kind of poem is this? Describe the sound pattern in the poem and why it's important.   the last words on lines 1,
2, 5

It is limerick, first 3 tres rhyme (Joe, slow, go)
and so does line 3+4. The poems rhyme is
to make it silly and funny for readers.

_____

Question 8

Hoot, alive at night,
Swoops down and preys on dinner.
Keeps watch, golden eyes.

In this poem, what animal is the poet talking about? Explain how you know this.

The poet is talking about an bird due to characterse which includes 'hoots', and it comes 'alive at night' this simplies that this bird is one owl.

Question 9

Match the type of literary text to its correct example.

TYPE OF TEXT   **EXAMPLE**

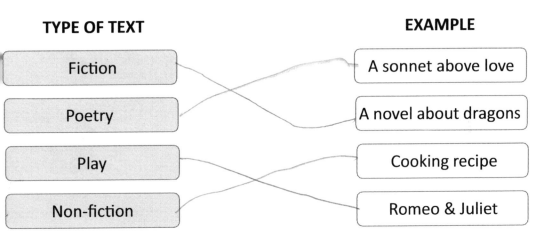

Fiction	A sonnet above love
Poetry	A novel about dragons
Play	Cooking recipe
Non-fiction	Romeo & Juliet

ANSWERS TO AUDIENCE, PURPOSE AND CONTEXT

Question 1

TEXT		AUDIENCE
School newsletter		Adults
A Science textbook		Cooking enthusiasts
A picture book		Students
A bakery magazine		Parents/guardians
A business letter		Children

Question 2

a) Adults / employees

The content of the speech is addressing people in a work place. The formal language that is used, shows that the text is being used in a professional environment.

b) Students

The language used in this sentence is also very formal. However, although it is addressing students (in an exam room), the formal language is used to emphasise the importance/seriousness of the situation.

c) Newspaper readers / adults

The language used clearly emphasises that this text has been taken from a newspaper article. This is informing the readers of current affairs/situations that are occurring.

Question 3

TEXT	PURPOSE OF TEXT
Cartoon programme	Entertainment
Weather report	Inform
An advert for a theme park opening	Persuade
Log book of science experiment	Explain
Debate about school uniforms	Argue
Leaflet on benefits of eating healthily	Advise

Question 4

a) The purpose of entertainment texts is to allow the reader/audience to feel joy and escapism.

b) The purpose of information texts is to provide the reader with information about a particular topic. This will improve their understanding and give them further insight into information that they may not have had.

c) Persuasion texts are used to try and persuade the reader to believe a certain viewpoint. These texts may also persuade readers/audience to actively do something.

d) Explanation texts are used to show "why" something happens. It uses examples and evidence to describe the events.

e) Argument texts offer the reader alternative viewpoints about the same topic.

f) Advice texts are used to help the reader make a decision about something by offering suggestions and opinions.

Question 5

You would expect to see images of the film industry. A magazine cover will usually have a main image to capture the audience's attention. Critic reviews, ratings and sub-headings would also be used to show the reader what the magazine contains. The purpose of the text is to provide information about films.

Question 6

a) The targeted reader for the text, *Persuasion*, is most probably readers who enjoy classic, old-fashioned storylines. We can assume that her targeted demographic is mostly women, due to the plotlines and strong female characters conveyed in the text.

b) The male and female roles are very defined. Back then, men were the 'bread winners' who would go out to work and provide for their family, whereas the women would stay at home, cleaning, cooking and raising the children.

c) The public domain focuses on going out to work, whereas the domestic domain focuses on household chores and raising the children. Austen contrasts the domains by suggesting that men are not fit for the latter.

d) The attitude of society, with men going out to work and women staying at home, has changed considerably over the time. Women now play a more active role, and go out to work, whereas men now take responsibilities within their homes.

Question 7

The sound pattern of this poem is extremely rhythmic. It is a limerick poem, which uses rhymes and rhythms with the intention of being funny or silly. The last words on the first, second and fifth row rhyme (Joe, slow and go). The third and fourth row also rhyme (race and pace).

Question 8

In this poem, the poet is talking about an owl. We know this because the language in the poem shows characteristics of an owl. For example, the use of the word "hoot" is the sound an owl makes. "Alive at night" indicates that it is an animal which is awake during the night. "Keeps watch, golden eyes" is describing the look of an owl, which has huge, golden eyes.

Question 9

| TYPE OF TEXT | EXAMPLE |

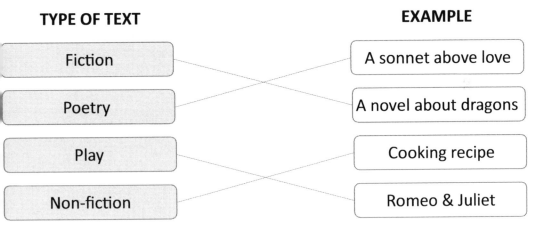

TYPE OF TEXT

Fiction

Poetry

Play

Non-fiction

EXAMPLE

A sonnet above love

A novel about dragons

Cooking recipe

Romeo & Juliet

HOW ARE YOU GETTING ON?

THE
REVISION
SERIES

LANGUAGE

(Critical Readings)

LANGUAGE

WHAT IS CRITICAL READING?

Reading a text critically simply means to understand the context and its value.

Generally, to examine a text critically, you would consider the following questions:

- What evidence is present?
- What is the main argument of the text?
- What is the author trying to convey?
- What language and/or literary techniques are used?
- What can I interpret from the text?
- Are there any influences?

> Reading critically does NOT always mean being negative/critical towards the text.

CHOOSING YOUR WORDS CAREFULLY

A writer will choose their words carefully when writing their text.

They will need to choose words which relate to the wider <u>purpose</u> of the text, and <u>audience</u> that they are addressing.

FAIRYTALES

This would use very simple language.
It would use lots of colourful, large images.
This makes it easier for children to read and keep them engaged with the story.

For more information on audience and purpose, please check out page 46.

LANGUAGE

INFORMAL VS. FORMAL

Informal and formal language are very different, and you would use these in very different writings.

INFORMAL LANGUAGE – this would mostly be used with friends or family members. Slang is classed as informal language. For example, a personal diary would probably use informal language.

FORMAL LANGUAGE – this would be used for more serious writing including professional and academic work. This would include newspaper reports and university essays.

FIGURATIVE LANGUAGE

Writers use figurative language in order to emphasise a particular point in more depth, or describe something or someone in a particular way.

FIGURATIVE LANGUAGE	EXPLANATION
Metaphors	Describing something 'as' something. This creates imagery. *E.g. The class was a zoo.*
Simile	Describing something 'like' or 'as' something else. This creates imagery. *E.g. As white as a sheep.*
Alliteration	Several words that repeat the same first letter. *E.g. Slow Sam Saw Shadows.*
Personification	Words that describe something with person or animal-like features. *E.g. The wind howled through the night.*
Hyperbole	An unrealistic comparison. Also known as exaggeration. *E.g. I am so hungry I could eat a horse.*
Onomatopoeia	These are words that 'sound' like what it is talking about. *E.g. The thunder rumbles through the night.*

LANGUAGE

HOW LANGUAGE CREATES MOOD AND ATMOSPHERE

Writers are very careful about what language they use in order to create meaning. They want their readers to <u>feel</u> a particular way.

<u>How is feeling created in a written text?</u>

There are several ways a writer can make their readers feel a particular way:

- Choice of vocabulary;
- Literary techniques including metaphors and similes;
- Punctuation including exclamation marks and ellipses;
- Sentence structure.

Look out for words that convey emotion
(triumphant, optimism, shock, gloomy)

Look out for punctuation
(It was epic!) = magnifies the sentence
(I was on the edge of my seat…) = creates suspense

Look out for metaphors and similes.
(His body turned to ice) = suggests fear.

As you can see, language is clearly important in any literary text.

Everything that has been written has been written on purpose. The writer carefully chooses their words in order to create meaning.

PRACTICE QUESTIONS

Question 1

Give a definition of the following, using an example sentence for each.

a) METAPHOR

describes something as something

Example

~~Ha~~ His hair was a lions mane

b) SIMILE

Describing something `like` or `as` something else

Example

As fast as lighting

c) PERSONIFICATION

Giving human actions to objects

Example

The waves breathed in and out

d) HYPERBOLE

An unrealistic comparison. Also known as exaggeration

Example

"I've told you this a million times."

Question 2

Below are four examples of a text, each having a different purpose. Circle all of the words that show which language would be most suitable for each purpose.

a) An academic paper

(FORMAL)   TECHNICAL   SLANG   INFORMAL   SIMPLE

b) A children's novel

FORMAL   TECHNICAL   SLANG   INFORMAL   (SIMPLE)

c) A letter to a close friend or relative

FORMAL   TECHNICAL   (SLANG)   (INFORMAL)   SIMPLE

d) A business presentation

(FORMAL   TECHNICAL)   SLANG   INFORMAL   SIMPLE

Question 3

For the following sentences, write whether the sentence is an example of any of the following:

Simile Metaphor Personification Hyperbole Alliteration Onomatopoeia

a) The traffic whizzed past me.   _Onomatopoeia_

b) I have a million things to do today.   _Hyp Hyperbole_

c) A rollercoaster of emotions.   _Pers Metaphor_

d) The fire ran wild.   _Personification_

e) Pete's parrot pranced proudly.   _Alliteration_

f) Blind as a bat.   _Simile_

Question 4

Read the passage and answer the following questions.

Strand by strand, Webster created an articulate infrastructure; a structure so defined and carefully constructed, that it made all others seem unrefined. Clear light lines that, although appeared fragile and breakable, were actually a strong, valuable asset to the world in which he lived.

"It's all in the spinning," Webster smiled as he continued to finish off his masterpiece. There was nothing Webster liked doing more than spending time with his companion, Toby. Together they would create a sense of security and triumph - Webster's definition of perfection.

On the surface, Webster appeared to be like any other of his kind; a dark shade of brown, with legs as fast as they could carry. Webster was just ordinary, nothing special, nothing different; just blending in with the rest of the crowd.

Webster and his Journey Home by How2Become

a) Explain how the use of language allows the reader to know that Webster is a spider.

The language used in this extract suggests to allow the reader that Webster is a spider. The verb 'spinning' combined with the phrase 'strand-by-strand' represent the making of a spider web.

b) Why do you think the writer chooses to use language that does not actually state Webster as being a spider?

The writer uses this language to describe Webster as a spider as it creates imagery at descriptive which makes the reader want to read onwards to find out who Webster is.

c) Describe the contrast in language between the first and third paragraph.

The contrast in language is shown as he has made a 'fragile [...], strong, valuable asset to the world' but he is just 'ordinary, nothing special, [...] just blending in'

Question 5

Read the passage and answer the following questions.

> She might have been absolutely rich and perfectly healthy, and yet be happy. Her spring of felicity was in the glow of her spirits, as her friend Anne's was in the warmth of her heart. Anne was tenderness itself, and she had the full worth of it in Captain Wentworth's affection. His profession was all that could ever make her friends wish that tenderness less, the dread of a future war all that could dim her sunshine. She gloried in being a sailor's wife, but she must pay the tax of quick alarm for belonging to that profession which is, if possible, more distinguished in its domestic virtues than in its national importance.
>
> *Persuasion by Jane Austen*

a) In this final paragraph of the novel, Austen is talking about the implications of being married to a Naval Officer. Describe how the use of language suggests that the Navy has an impact upon marriage.

The language used ~~show~~ suggests that it is ~~harder~~ difficult to be married to someone in the Navy. As although this women may ~~have be~~ 'rich' and 'healthy' she ~~is~~ always has a constant fear of losing her husband

b) Austen is articulate in her choice of words. Using an example from the passage, explain how Austen provides recognition and respect to the Navy.

_____

_____

_____

_____

_____

Question 6

Read the passage and answer the following questions.

There seemed to be no use in waiting by the little door, so she went back to the table, half hoping she might find another key on it, or at any rate a book of rules for shutting people up like telescopes: this time she found a little bottle on it, ('which certainly was not here before,' said Alice,) and round the neck of the bottle was a paper label with the words 'DRINK ME' beautifully printed on it in large letters.

It was all very well to say 'Drink me,' but the wise, little Alice was not going to do *that* in a hurry. 'No I'll look first,' she said, 'and see whether it's marked *"poison"* or not:' for she had read several nice little histories about children who had got burnt, and eaten up by wild beasts and other unpleasant things, all because they *would* not remember the simple rules their friends had taught them: such as, that a red-hot poker will burn you if you hold it too long; and that if you cut your finger *very* deeply with a knife, it usually bleeds; and she had never forgotten that, if you drink much from a bottle marked 'poison,' it is almost certain to disagree with you, sooner or later.

However, this bottle was *not* marked 'poison,' so Alice ventured to taste it and finding it very nice, (it had, in fact, a sort of mixed flavour of cherry-tart, custard, pine-apple, roast turkey, toffee, and hot buttered toast,) she very soon finished it off.

'What a curious feeling!' said Alice; 'I must be shutting up like a telescope.'

Alice's Adventures in Wonderland by Lewis Carroll

a) The author of this book portrays Alice as a curious little girl. Using an example from the text, explain how the author's language shapes our views about Alice.

Alice can be described as a curious young girl who seeks adventures, this is show with the adjectives 'curious' combined with the verb 'ventured'

b) The author makes reference to changes in Alice's physical description. Using **examples** from the text, why do you think the author does this and what does this tell us about the character of Alice?

_____

_____

_____

_____

c) Write a simile from the text and explain what it means.

_____

_____

_____

_____

d) Carroll explores this idea of escapism and unlocking dreams and fantasies. Explain how the 'key' is symbolic to these themes, and analyse why the author has used this language in order to convey a sense of surrealism.

_____

_____

_____

_____

_____

_____

_____

_____

ANSWERS TO LANGUAGE

Question 1

a) A metaphor is a figure of speech which is applied to something that is not literally applicable. For example, 'the apple of my eye' is a metaphor. Of course, there is no apple in the eye. Instead, the apple represents a person who is loved and admired.

b) A simile is a figure of speech that uses words or phrases to describe something being 'like' or 'as' something else. For example, 'cute as a kitten' is a simile. Similes use the words 'like' or 'as' to describe one thing as something else.

c) Personification is using words to describe things using human or animal-like qualities. For example, 'the wind howled during the night'. The wind does not actually 'howl', instead it is describing the sound of the wind using animal-like qualities.

d) Hyperboles are extreme exaggerations about something in order to make something seem more excessive. For example, 'I'm so hungry I could eat a horse'. This is clearly an exaggeration of how hungry that person is.

Question 2

a) Formal and technical

b) Informal and simple

c) Informal, slang and simple

d) Formal and technical

Question 3

a) Onomatopoeia

b) Hyperbole

c) Metaphor

d) Personification

e) Alliteration

f) Simile

Question 4

a) The use of language clearly suggests that Webster is a spider. The use of the words 'strand by strand', 'spinning' and 'a structure so defined and carefully constructed' all represent the makings of a spider web.

b) The writer uses language that does not actually state Webster as being a spider because it allows the reader to be provided with details without actually stating what or who it is. This makes it more appealing to readers as they will want to continue reading to find out who Webster is.

c) The difference in language between the first and third paragraphs is the use of colour. In the first paragraph, 'clear light lines' contrast with the 'dark shade of brown' in the third paragraph. This creates visual imagery for the reader and allows the reader to understand the different elements of a spider and its web.

Question 5

a) The use of language regarding marriage suggests the difficulties in being married to someone in the Navy. It suggests that a woman cannot be truly happy in her marriage due to the constant worry and fear of her husband serving his country.

b) The final line 'if possible, more distinguished in its domestic virtues than in its national importance' reinforces Austen's admiration and respect for the Navy. She recognises the importance of the Navy on a national spectrum, which signifies how language is important in distinguishing both the downsides of Navy life in regards to marriage, but important to the rest of society.

Question 6

a) Alice can be described as a curious young girl who is seeking an exciting new adventure. This is demonstrated through the use of words such as, "curious" and "ventured".

b) The author conveys Alice's character in different sizes – small and normal-sized. This is emphasised when she drinks the potion and shrinks to "ten inches tall". The author does this to illustrate fantasy; "I must be shutting up like a telescope". This could not happen in real life and therefore it's all in the imagination. The author might have done this to show that Alice is not comfortable with who she is. For example, she has to change into a different version of herself in order to find happiness.

c) The simile in the text is: "I must be shutting up like a telescope". This is most likely referring to making someone smaller. "Shutting up" doesn't necessarily mean to make someone quiet, but to "shut up" i.e. to make smaller, like a telescope when its put away after being used.

d) The key could be used as a symbol for Alice's imagination. Alice is trying to unlock the door to enter a world of pure imagination. The door could represent the barrier between real life and fantasy. It could also represent the entrance and exit to happiness; opening up new experiences and adventures. This reinforces the idea of surrealism, and how Alice uses the 'little' door as a way of escaping into a world of fantasy.

HOW ARE YOU GETTING ON?

CHARACTERS, NARRATIVE AND STRUCTURE

(Critical Readings)

CHARACTERS, NARRATIVE AND STRUCTURE

When reading a text, particularly a story, it is important to pay attention to the <u>characters</u> involved.

UNDERSTANDING CHARACTERISATION

Writers use characters as a way of making their story more engaging.

Without good, strong, recognisable characters, a narrative would not work – no matter how strong the story is!

KING	FAIRY	ROBBER
Characterisation	**Characterisation**	**Characterisation**
• *Wealthy*	• *Good*	• *Evil*
• *Power*	• *Caring*	• *Villain*
• *Greed*	• *Loyalty*	• *Greed*
• *Authority*	• *Kindness*	• *Immoral*

When it comes to reading and writing, it is important that you not only describe the characters, but you use language to emphasise their characterisation.

For example, what the character says will go a long way in determining how they come across to readers.

Remember, the <u>voice</u> of the story is important. This might not necessarily be the characters, but also the voice of the narrator/author.

Consider the following when looking at characterisation:

- *How are the characters dressed?*
- *How do they behave?*
- *What is the feeling of the narrator?*
- *Who is telling the story?*
- *What different types of characters are used and why?*

CHARACTERS, NARRATIVE AND ST

As well as characters, writers also put a lot of thought structure, and themes.

NARRATIVE

One of the most important things in relation to literary texts, es   ₋ıs, is the narrative.

Narrative is another way of saying 'storyline'.

The narrative will all depend on what type of text it is and who the writer's reader is going to be.

When thinking of a narrative, it is important to consider the following:

- *Who is telling the story? Is it in 1st person or 3rd person?*
- *Can you work out the beginning, middle and end of the story?*
- *What is the overall message of the story?*
- *What is the importance of the story?*
- *Does the author want you to be feeling a certain way?*

CREATING A NARRATIVE

Behind every great book is a strong narrative that draws the reader in, and captures a story that is thrilling and appealing to its targeted readers.

The narrative is where the author can get really creative. Remember, fiction writing is all about make-believe. Therefore, the ideas and imagination behind these stories can be completely unrealistic and wacky.

CHARACTERS, NARRATIVE AND STRUCTURE

THEMES

This ties in with narrative. Themes will appear throughout a story. The author will have created at least one theme in their writing.

Basically, a theme is an idea which the author wants you to consider. These themes could be any of the following:

Family	Loyalty	Love	Betrayal
Power	Time	Conflict	Fear
Coming-of-Age	Redemption	Death	Religion
Discovery	Freedom	Good vs. Evil	Greed

Different authors place different emphasis on different themes in order to convey a certain message or idea.

Some themes are really obvious, whilst others are quite subtle. The author does this on purpose. They want you to think about what you have read, and get you to question the importance of the hidden morals and underlying themes.

OLIVER TWIST

The themes conveyed in Oliver Twist include:
- Suffering
- Poverty
- Hunger
- Society and class
- Identity
- Belonging

PRIDE AND PREJUDICE

The themes conveyed in Pride and Prejudice include:
- Love
- Reputation
- Class and social standing
- Family

TOP TIP!

When reading a text, make some notes about the key themes portrayed.

What is the author trying to convey? What messages are being put across the most?

Are there any subtle themes in the text?

CHARACTERS, NARRATIVE AND STRUCTURE

STRUCTURE AND LAYOUT

Texts are laid out in very specific ways in order to fit in with its purpose, and attract its audience.

Layout can vary from text to text. Things to look out for might be:

- Headers
- Bullet points
- Numbered lists

Example

The best example to convey the importance of layout is newspaper articles.

They use a very specific layout in order to attract their audience and serve their purpose.

Newspapers use columns as a way of making the text easier to read.

This allows large amounts of information to be broken up with the help of sub-headings and images.

Other texts, such as revision guides, would use sub-headings and textboxes as a way of separating different information in order to make it easier to learn the material.

Be sure you know the importance of the layout!

CHARACTERS, NARRATIVE AND STRUCTURE

THE IMPORTANCE OF STRUCTURE

The first thing you need to understand is that the structure of your story is important. It allows the reader to be engaged instantly, and be kept excited until the very end.

Every story has a beginning, middle and end:

BEGINNING

- Introducing your reader to your style of writing.
- Setting up the scene and introducing the main characters.
- Creating a 'situation' or 'problem' right at the beginning will make sure that your reader is instantly 'hooked'.
- You need to grab the reader's attention. Make it thrilling. Make it fast-paced. Make the reader want to continue reading.
- Don't give away all of the key details at the beginning. Provide your readers with enough information, so that they will want to continue reading on to find out more.

MIDDLE

- This is where the bulk of your story will take place.
- You need to hold the reader's attention by maintaining a plotline that is interesting, and will push the reader to finish the story.
- Develop obstacles and complications which the characters need to solve.
- Although there might be a few complications, your story should reach a CLIMAX or turning point.
- There is a massive situation which the main character has to try and resolve.
- A good middle will allow the reader to wonder how the story will end.

END

- This is where the climax or turning point of your story will become resolved.
- Your main character/s will have learnt a lesson, or come to terms with the events that have happened.
- A good ending will allow the reader to continue thinking about the story, even after finishing reading it.

If you are reading a non-fiction text, the structure of the text would be slightly different.

Remember to pay attention to the layout and structure of a text. This will help you to analyse what the author was trying to achieve, and how they have tried to appeal to their targeted audience.

PRACTICE QUESTIONS

Question 1

Read the passage carefully and answer the following questions.

WHAT IS A VOLCANO?

The origin of the word volcano comes from the word 'Vulcan' – a god of fire in Roman Mythology.

Most volcanoes are mountains and found in the Pacific Ocean. Magma and poisonous gases build up before exploding through the Earth's surface.

A volcano is a type of landform that opens downwards to a pool of molten rock (magma).

HOW ARE VOLCANOES FORMED?

The Earth has three layers – the crust (at the top), the mantle (the middle), and the core (the centre).

The formation of volcanoes is quite simple. When magma from below the Earth's upper mantle works its way to the surface, this creates an eruption.

DIFFERENT STAGES OF VOLCANOES

There are three main categories which define what kind of volcano it is – active, dormant and extinct.

An active volcano is a volcano that is or has erupted recently, and is likely to erupt again.

A dormant volcano is a volcano that has not erupted recently, but is likely to erupt.

An extinct volcano is a volcano that has not erupted and is not expected to erupt.

WHY DO VOLCANOES ERUPT?

Volcanoes erupt due to the friction between the plates of the Earth's crust. These 'tectonic plates' fit together like a jigsaw puzzle, and when these plates move, it causes the volcano to erupt.

Volcanoes are also suggested to trigger other natural disasters such as earthquakes, flooding, mud flows, rock falls and tsunamis.

EFFECTS OF VOLCANOES

Eruptions of volcanoes have long-lasting effects on both humans and the environment.

Some of the consequences following a volcano eruption include:

- Destroyed buildings;

- Destroyed habitats and landscapes;

- People becoming homeless;

- People being killed or seriously injured;

- Ash covering plants, making them inedible;

- Poisonous gases killing people and animals;

- Dark skies, strong winds and heavy rain may follow.

THE MAUNA LOA

The Mauna Loa (meaning Long Mountain) is the largest active shield volcano in the world. That means it's built almost entirely of fluid magma flows.

This volcano is one of five that forms the Island of Hawaii in the Pacific Ocean.

Having erupted over 33 times since 1843, the Mauna Loa is taller than Mount Everest if measured from its base below sea level to its summit.

a) What kind of text do you think this text is taken from? Explain your answer.

This extract is th taken from an articale, the columns makes it easier to reads. abot volcaneos.

b) Why do you think the writer has used a question as the first sub-heading?

The writer uses a question to as sub heading as it draws the reader to in to find the answer.

c) Why do you think the writer has put the paragraphs 'What is a volcano?' and 'How are volcanoes formed?' next to each other?

So any The writer has done this, so if there are any questions they will be answered.

d) Explain why the layout of the bullet points is useful in a text like this.

Bullet points are used to space out the writing and so it doesn't confuse people when reading.

e) Write a couple of sentences about why the writer has produced this piece of literary text.

The writer has produced this piece of text, to let po allow people to know more information at about volcaneos.

f) Why do you think the writer has listed the effects of volcanoes? How does this appeal to its reader?

As there are more effects leang consequences to a volcaneo erupting, it shows the reader the danger of ce volkaneo

Question 2

Below are two different passages, each laid out in a very particular way. Look at the passages and answer the following questions.

Do you warm-up before exercise?
A warm-up is really important **before** you exercise. You need to get your muscles and body prepared for the exercise that you are about to undergo.

The aim of a warm-up is to:
- Prevent injury.
- Prepare the body for exercise.
- Allow for greater flexibility and range of movement.
- Increase heart rate and blood flow in order for your muscles to react quicker.

Stage 1 – light jog   5-10 minutes

State 2 – stretches   Paying particular focus to what areas you are going to be exercising the most.

Stage 3 – skills activities   Practice skills to warm up the muscles used in the main activity.

Stage 4 – mental preparation   Visualising the end goal.

UNEXPLAINED OBJECT IN BRITISH SKIES

A BIZARRE, UNIDENTIFIED object was once again reported soaring the skies right here in Britain.

Two reports were made on the very same day and were claimed to have happened just minutes apart. Paranormal experts and scientific investigators are staggered by this profound event, and are furthering their inquiries.

The first incident was reported at 08:16am on Wednesday, and the unnamed witness claims to have been "fetching her daily newspaper" when the extraordinary thing happened. She claims that she's "never seen anything like it" and "had to look twice".

A flying object, which was described by both witnesses as being triangular-shaped, was caught flying through the skies over the countryside in Lenham, Kent.

The next reporting was at 09:32am, 2,000 miles south from the first location.

Sammie Harris, 26, and her husband, Daniel, 29, were driving back to their house, when they both looked out the passenger-side window. Sammie pulled over the car, and they both stepped out.

"It was a flat object, a light colour, which drifted through the air. Like a shooting star falling from the sky, the object appeared to be heading downwards", Daniel claimed, with both nerves and excitement in his voice.

"If my husband had not been there, I don't think anyone would have believed me". Sammie was unsure what she saw at first, and when she pointed it out to Daniel, they both came to the same conclusion.

All of the witnesses described the object as having a slight yellow tinge to it, which flashed in time with a regular heartbeat.

Neither of the witnesses were able to film nor capture the event on camera.

a) What is the purpose of Item 1?

Informs & instrust how to warm up, also includes benifets and examples

b) What kind of text is Item 2 taken from? Explain how you know this based on layout and structure.

_____

_____

_____

_____

_____

c) In Item 1, why do you think the writer has provided information in textboxes?

_____

_____

_____

d) In Item 1, why do you think the writer uses bullet points?

_____

_____

_____

e) In Item 2, why do you think the first two words in the first paragraph are written in capital letters?

_____

_____

_____

f) Why do you think the writer of Item 1 uses a question as its first sentence?

_____

_____

_____

_____

_____

Question 3

For this story, your title is 'The Eye'. What you need to do is fill in the boxes below, in order to come up with a plan for a possible narrative.

This is a great way to practice reading and writing. Understanding how to write something, will give you some indication as to how other writers go about writing their stories.

IDEAS

THEMES / MOTIFS

CHARACTERS

SETTINGS

NARRATIVE

ANSWERS TO CHARACTERS, NARRATIVE AND STRUCTURE

Question 1

a) This text is taken from an article. It uses columns as a way of making the paragraphs clear and easy to read. The text is informative as it is teaching you facts about volcanoes – it is documenting information about a particular subject. It uses technical language, facts and diagrams to inform its reader about the topic.

b) The writer has used a question as the first sub-heading as it instantly draws in the reader and makes them question the content being conveyed.

c) The writer has placed these two paragraphs next to one another because they both discuss the formations of a volcano and how they work. Therefore, the paragraphs are closely linked to one another.

d) The bullet points help to provide easy to read information quickly. They separate information by listing the content as examples, which stand out to the reader.

e) The writer has wrote this literary text as a way of informing their readers about a particular topic. It is a topic that raises many questions which are answered in this article.

f) The writer has listed the effects volcanoes have because it allows the reader to understand how volcanoes can impact not only humans, but the environment. This allows the reader to feel empathy towards the victims of volcanic eruptions.

Question 2

a) The purpose of Item 1 is to instruct and inform readers on how to successfully warm-up. It provides the benefits of warming up before exercising, and shows examples of how to warm up effectively.

b) This is a newspaper article. You know that it is a newspaper article because the writing is separated into columns, which is a common feature of newspaper articles. It also has one main heading and an image to go alongside the article.

c) The information in the textboxes are there to provide additional information to the reader.

d) The bullet points are used to provide clear, simple sentences regarding the benefits of warming up. This makes this information stand out, which makes it visually enticing.

e) The first two words are written in capital letters in order to draw the reader into the content of the article. The words 'bizarre' and 'unidentified' create a sense of mystery, which automatically makes the article seem interesting.

f) The writer uses a question as the first sentence, because it is directly talking to the reader. It automatically draws them in by asking them if they warm up before they exercise. This makes the text interactive.

Question 3

The aim of this task is to practice your writing skills. This will allow you to understand how writers go about writing their text.

When reading a text, you need to focus on many literary elements, which allow the text to appeal to its reader.

You could have come up with any information so long as it ties in with the title of the story, 'The Eye'.

Consider the following:

- What are the main ideas behind the story?
- What is going to happen?
- What is the overall aim of the story?
- What themes are going to occur? Are there any underlying themes/motifs?
- Who is the protagonist?
- What other characters are going to appear?
- Think about characterisation.
- What role do they play in the story?
- Where is the story set?
- Where will the main events take place?
- What is the narrative?
- Consider how the story is going to begin, the events of the story, and the ending.
- How do you want your reader to feel?

HOW ARE YOU GETTING ON?

THE REVISION SERIES

COMPARING TEXTS

COMPARING TEXTS

WHY DO YOU HAVE TO COMPARE?

Sometimes, you will be required to look at more than one text and compare them.

In order to do this, you will need to look at the <u>similarities</u> and <u>differences</u>.

- *What language do they use?*
- *Do the texts have the same purpose?*
- *Do the texts have the same subject?*
- *Do they use similar techniques?*
- *How do the texts differ?*
- *How are the texts the same?*
- *Do they have different viewpoints or ideas?*

DRAWING COMPARISONS

TOP TIP!

Imagine you are a detective. You need to pick out all of the little details in order to form a solid conclusion.

WRITE ABOUT THE TEXTS TOGETHER

When you compare texts, you want to avoid talking about one and then the other.

You should talk about one aspect and talk about both texts, drawing examples from both texts.

Things you should compare might be:

Language	Purpose	Meaning	Opinions
Setting	Structure	Layout	Audience
Mood	Perspective	Aim	Style

PRACTICE QUESTIONS

Question 1

Compare and contrast the rhythm and structure of at least two poems.

POEM 1
Hoot, alive at night,
Swoops down and preys on dinner.
Keeps watch, golden eyes.

POEM 2
The crazy weather,
Lightning strikes the black, night sky.
Unpredictable.

POEM 3
Winter's icy grip,
My fingers as cold as ice.
Building a snow fort,
To escape, to dream, to hope.
Frozen moment, strong silence.

POEM 4
Wind – an angry witch.
Thunder strikes and lights the sky,
Nature's breathing wild.
Trees thrashed and the air whistled,
Like turbulence on a plane.

Question 2

Compare and contrast the sound imagery in both the 'Countryside by Day' and 'City by Night'. What do you think the poets are trying to convey?

COUNTRYSIDE BY DAY	CITY BY NIGHT
Deep into the woods, where nothing is heard, Except for the humming of an invisible bird. Not a sound, nor whisper, nor spoken word. An oak tree wrinkled for a 100 years, The perfect post to shed your tears. Supportive and strong - like it appears. Next to the tree flowed a crystal clear stream, A vision of beauty, a waking dream. The yellow rays that beat and beamed. Peaceful bliss, so solitude, All my thoughts and ideas persued. A place to think, a place to view. These are the things the countryside bring, Butterfly wings and birds that sing. As precious as a royalty's ring. High tree tops that offer protection, A perfect time for self-reflection. The sounds and wildlife is perfection. A countryside by day.	Walking along 1st avenue, The sky above all dark and blue. Hidden from the colourful lights, Stars forbidden to shine so bright. A city of people sleeping away, Sleeping soundly, awaiting for day. To me, though, the best part is the night, Manhattan's magic comes into sight. A city of life, and a city of beat, The music that fills the lit-up street. Never dull, never alone, Never silent, never a drone. A city of experience like I have never seen, The energy, the vibes, the almighty gleam. Everyone always moving fast-paced, Yet they move with poise, they move with grace. The city sounds heard after dark, Buzzed through the empty, childless park. Dreams, fantasies and hope to achieve, Makes me never want to leave. A city by night.

Question 3

Compare the reviews on two plays of William Shakespeare.

REVIEW OF ROMEO AND JULIET (opening night)

Shakespeare at his best; this play contains everything you would want to see in theatre – romance, violence, tension, sacrifice!

A noble attempt to bring the wonders of Shakespeare to life. The cast were truly exceptional, and the director did an outstanding job in finding the right actor for each role.

The clever dialogue and beautiful poetry all tied in with the beauty of each scene. Great thought went into every element of the play, and this clearly showed in the opening night.

REVIEW OF ROMEO AND JULIET (the last night)

After reading great reviews about the opening night, I had psyched myself up for a night full of conflict, love, violence and poetry.

However, this "noble attempt" did not live up to my expectation. The modern-day twist which was put on the classic love story simply did not work.

The characters were abysmal and put in little effort. Maybe they were tired from all their shows, or maybe their acting was just not up to par with what I would expect from professionals.

a) Write a sentence that sums up the overall views of both reviewers.

_____

_____

_____

b) Compare the language used in both of the reviews and how this creates a difference in interpretation.

_____

_____

_____

c) Why does review 2 use a quote from review 1? How does he use this quote and to what effect?

_____

_____

_____

Question 4

Give four ways you can compare texts.

1. _____

2. _____

3. _____

4. _____

Question 5

Based on the two reviews, explain why audiences may have different views on the same thing.

_____

_____

_____

_____

_____

_____

ANSWERS TO COMPARING TEXTS

Question 1

Poems 1 and 2 are the same in structure and rhythm. They both follow the structure of a haiku poem. A haiku is a type of Japanese poem, which uses 3 lines. The syllable pattern of a haiku is 5 / 7 / 5. Both poems 1 and 2 follow this pattern.

For example, the first line should have five syllables ("Hoot, alive at night" and "The crazy weather"). The second line should have seven syllables ("Swoops down and preys on dinner" and "Lightning strikes the black night sky.") And finally, the third line should have five syllables ("Keeps watch, golden eyes" and "Unpredictable".)

Question 2

The sound imagery conveyed in the poems are very different to one another. In the 'City by Night' it explores 'music' and 'beat' which creates an upbeat image. Whereas in the 'Countryside of Day', the sound imagery is conveyed as being 'peaceful bliss' and where 'nothing is heard'. The poets are trying to contrast day with night, by comparing a world of solitude and peace with an upbeat life.

Question 3

a) The overall view of review 1 is extremely optimistic. The reviewer enjoyed the play and is complimentary about the narrative and characters. Review 2 has a completely different outlook on the play and describes it as being a disappointment.

b) Review 1 uses uplifting language including "best", "noble attempt" and "truly exceptional". This demonstrates that the reviewer enjoyed the play. Comparatively, the language in review 2 is quite hostile. The reviewer uses language such as "did not live up to my expectation", "abysmal" and "little effort". This reinforces how the choice of words is important, in order to convey a particular viewpoint.

c) Review 2 quotes from review 1 and puts it in speech marks. This reinforces that he does not believe it to be a "noble attempt", and in actual fact, the reviewer thinks the exact opposite.

Question 4

1. Language
2. Audience
3. Structure
4. Themes

Question 5

It is important to understand who the text is being aimed at. For example, the play of Romeo and Juliet is only going to appeal to specific people; it is not going to appeal to everyone. Therefore, age, sex, social status could all be influencing factors in regards to whether a literary text appeals to someone or not.

HOW ARE YOU GETTING ON?

THE
REVISION
SERIES

INTRODUCTION
TO SHAKESPEARE

WILLIAM SHAKESPEARE

WHO IS WILLIAM SHAKESPEARE?

William Shakespeare is a famous British poet and playwright, and is still considered one of the greatest writers in literary history.

SHAKESPEARE AND HIS WORK

Shakespeare wrote around 40 plays, 154 sonnets and a whole range of other poetry.

Some of his most well-known plays include:

Romeo and Juliet	Macbeth	Julius Caesar
A Midsummer Night's Dream	The Taming of the Shrew	Much Ado About Nothing
King Lear	Hamlet	Othello

The works of Shakespeare are taught in schools as a way of recognising writing that is in an old-fashioned style.

Due to the time in which Shakespeare was writing (over 400 years ago), his writing style is very different to how we read and write today.

Looking at Shakespeare is a great way for children to learn the importance of language in relation to context. The time in which something is written has great bearing on the writing style which is used. Some modern authors use old-fashioned writing techniques to emphasise that their writing is being placed during a different time period.

WILLIAM SHAKESPEARE

TYPES OF SHAKESPEAREAN PLAYS

There are three types of Shakespearean plays:

1. Comedies
2. Tragedies
3. Histories

Comedies

- This is a different type of humour than what we find funny in today's world.
- Most Shakespearean comedies offer dramatic storylines, alongside their underlying humour.
- Most comedies offer a happy ending.

Characteristics = struggle of young love, element of separation, mistaken identities, interwoven plotlines, use of puns and irony and family conflict/tension.

Tragedies

- Tend to be more serious, dramatic and tense.
- Usually involve death of main character/s.

Characteristics = social breakdown, isolation of main characters, ends in death, noble characters who are brought down by their flaws and no escape from the drama.

Histories

- Focus on English monarchs including King John, Richard II, Henry VIII and loads more.
- Use of Elizabethan propaganda.
- Dangers of civil war and conflict.
- Present a particular image of monarchs, although often considered as misrepresentations and inaccurate.

Characteristics = use of English monarchs to centre the storyline, glorify ancestors, depict monarchs in a particular way, and use conflict and tragedy to dramatise the narrative.

WILLIAM SHAKESPEARE

THE USE OF LANGUAGE

Many people struggle to understand the works of Shakespeare, because his writing style and language is extremely different to ours.

The use of old-fashioned language made it difficult for readers to interpret, but these words and phrases were often worked out by understanding the rest of the script.

<u>Example from Macbeth</u>:

> **MACBETH**
> To-night we hold a solemn supper sir,
> And I'll request your presence.
>
> **BANQUO**
> Let your highness
> Command upon me; to the which my duties
> Are with a most indissoluble tie
> For ever knit.
>
> **MACBETH**
> Ride you this afternoon?
>
> **BANQUO**
> Ay, my good lord.

Shakespeare also used poetry techniques in his plays. The characters in his plays would sometimes speak in a poetic form, and this allowed the play to gain rhythm and pace in regards to language and dialogue.

UNDERSTANDING THE CHARACTERS

You need to have a good understanding of the characters, and understand how their portrayal is significant to the overall narrative.

There are three things that you need to consider when analysing the characters:

1. What they say;
2. How they behave;
3. The way they look.

Understanding the characters is important, because it allows the reader/audience to understand why they do things, and how this links to the overall themes of the play.

- *What do characters say to themselves? What do they say to others? How do they say it?*
- *What are they up to? What are they trying to do?*
- *How do they relate to the reader/audience?*
- *What motifs are established from each character?*
- *How do the characters look?*
- *How significant is their role to the overall narrative?*

For more practice questions on Shakespeare, check out our KS3 Shakespeare guide:

MARILYN
SHEPHERD

PRACTICE QUESTIONS

ACT II   Scene II *(Capulet's orchard).*

[Juliet appears above at a window]

ROMEO. But soft! what light through yonder window breaks?
It is the east and Juliet is the sun.
Arise, fair sun, and kill the envious moon,
Who is already sick and pale with grief
That thou, her maid, art far more fair than she.
Be not her maid, since she is envious;
Her vestal livery is but sick and green,

And none but fools do wear it. Cast it off!
It is my lady, O, it is my love!
O that she knew she were!
She speaks, yet she says nothing; what of that?
Her eye discourses, I will answer it.
I am too bold: 'tis not to me she speaks.
Two of the fairest stars in all the heaven,
Having some business, do entreat her eyes
To twinkle in their spheres till they return.
What if her eyes were there, they in her head?
The brightness of her cheek would shame those stars,
As daylight doth a lamp. Her eyes in heaven
Would through the airy region stream so bright
That birds would sing and think it were not night.
See how she leans her cheek upon her hand.
O that I were a glove upon that hand,
That I might touch that cheek!

JULIET. Ay me!

ROMEO. She speaks. *(Aside)*
O, speak again, bright angel, for thou art
As glorious to this night, being o'er my head,
As is a winged messenger of heaven
Unto the white-upturned wondering eyes
Of mortals that fall back to gaze on him

Romeo and Juliet

Question 1

What do you think Shakespeare is talking about when he uses the term "winged messenger"?

Question 2

Find a quote which highlights how Romeo compares Juliet to the stars. What does this mean in terms of his feelings for her?

Question 3

Shakespeare contrasts day with night. What do you think this means in terms of Romeo and Juliet's relationship?

Question 4

Romeo is standing in Juliet's garden. What could the garden symbolise in terms of motifs and themes?

ACT II   Scene II

*Enter **Macbeth,** with bloody daggers*

LADY MACBETH.   My husband!

MACBETH.   I have done the deed. Didst thou not hear a noise?

LADY MACBETH.   I heard the owl scream and the crickets cry. Did not you speak?

MACBETH.   When?

LADY MACBETH.   Now.

MACBETH.   As I descended?

LADY MACBETH.   Ay.

MACBETH.   Hark! Who lies i' th' second chamber?

LADY MACBETH.   Donalbain.

MACBETH.   *(looking at his hands)* This is a sorry sight.

LADY MACBETH.   A foolish thought, to say a sorry sight.

MACBETH.   There's one did laugh in's sleep, and one cried.
"Murder!"
That they did wake each other. I stood and heard them.
But they did say their prayers, and addressed them
Again to sleep.

LADY MACBETH.   There are two lodged together.

MACBETH.   One cried, "God bless us!" and "Amen" the other,
As they had seen me with these hangman's hands.
List'ning their fear I could not say "Amen,"
When they did say "God bless us!"

LADY MACBETH.   Consider it not so deeply.

Macbeth

Question 5

What do you think the author means by the phrase "hangman's hands"?

Question 6

Why do you think Macbeth was unable to say "Amen"? What does this say to the reader about the character of Macbeth?

Question 7

What does the word "descended" mean?

Question 8

The themes of death and violence are emphasised in this extract. What does this suggest about the rest of the narrative?

ANSWERS TO INTRODUCTION TO SHAKESPEARE

Question 1

The term "winged messenger" suggest angel-like features. Angels send messages down from heaven, and this is how Romeo sees Juliet, standing above him in the window.

Question 2

"Two of the fairest stars in all the heaven / Having some business do entreat her eyes". This suggests that Romeo sees Juliet as being bright and as beautiful as the stars above. It shows Romeo's love for Juliet by comparing her to something idyllic and beautiful.

Question 3

Shakespeare compares day and night in this scene in order to demonstrate the good and bad in Romeo and Juliet's lives. It emphasises opposing forces in their relationship. This suggests that Romeo and Juliet's relationship could be seen as a struggle or conflict.

Question 4

The garden could symbolise freedom, peace and love. It could also represent innocence and purity.

Question 5

The author uses the words "hangman's hands" to suggest that Macbeth's hands are bloody, and therefore he has committed a crime.

Question 6

Macbeth might not have been able to say "Amen" because he didn't want to wake them up. Also, he might not have been able to say it because he felt ashamed before God.

Question 7

The word "descended" means move or fall downwards.

Question 8

The themes of death and violence are highlighted in this extract. This suggests that Macbeth is a strong, masculine character who uses violence as a way of getting what he wants and showing who is in power. The image of Macbeth's bloody hands and carrying a dagger suggests his violent nature, as well as the lasting consequences of such actions. Therefore, it is possible to say that the narrative of the play is centred on these key ideas and themes.

NEED A LITTLE EXTRA HELP WITH KEY STAGE THREE (KS3) ENGLISH?

How2become have created other FANTASTIC guides to help you and your child prepare for their Key Stage Three (KS3) English.

FOR MORE INFORMATION ON OUR KEY STAGE 3 (KS3) GUIDES, PLEASE CHECK OUT THE FOLLOWING:

WWW.HOW2BECOME.COM

Get Access To

FREE

Psychometric Tests

www.PsychometricTestsOnline.co.uk

Printed in Great Britain
by Amazon

64882201R00070